FRANCIS FRITH'S

A Taste of the
SOUTH-WEST

REGIONAL RECIPES FROM THE SOUTH-WESTERN
COUNTIES OF ENGLAND

Illustrated with historical photographs from
The Francis Frith Collection

FRANCIS FRITH'S

A Taste of the
SOUTH-WEST

Swindon, Children Outside The Great Western Railway Works 1913 S254607

Compiled by Julia Skinner

First published in the United Kingdom by
The Francis Frith Collection exclusively for Oakridge in 2009.
Paperback Edition ISBN 978-1-84589-434-4

British Library Cataloguing in Publication Data

A Taste of the South-West
Julia Skinner

The Francis Frith Collection®
Frith's Barn, Teffont,
Salisbury, Wiltshire SP3 5QP
Tel: +44 (0) 1722 716 376
Email: info@francisfrith.co.uk
www.francisfrith.com

Printed and bound in Malta

Front Cover: **Plymouth, The Barbican 1890** 22474t
The colour-tinting in this image is for illustrative purposes only, and is not intended
to be historically accurate.

CONTENTS

INTRODUCTION

—·—

'If you in Do'set be a-roamen,

An' ha' business at a farm

Then won't ye see your eale a-foamen,

Or your cider down to warm?

Woon't ye have brown bread a-put ye?

An' some venny cheese ent ye?

Butter? Rolls o't!

Cream? Why bowls o't!'

A poem in the Dorset dialect by Reverend William Barnes (1800-86).

Travel around the south-western counties of England through the pages of this book and discover a selection of the delicious traditional food of the area, as well as some of the stories and fascinating facts behind the recipes. Your journey will be given added savour by the historical images taken by photographers from The Francis Frith Collection, showing the people and places of Avon, Cornwall, Devon, Dorset, Gloucestershire, Somerset and Wiltshire in the past.

Regional traditional dishes were developed from the local produce that was available to thrifty housewives who had to feed large, hungry families on a limited budget. Many of the old recipes also reflect the limited cookery techniques that were available in the past, as well as the skills of the cooks who were able to provide cheap and tasty meals with only a fire, a skillet and a cauldron to cook with, often producing the historical version of 'boil in the bag' meals.

This book is not intended to provide a comprehensive collection of the local recipes of the region, and some recipes are modern interpretations using some of the fine local produce that the area is famous for, but we hope that the food described within these pages, as well as the descriptions of traditional customs, local information and dialect words, will provide you with a taste of the south-west.

Newlyn, Fishermen 1906 56532

SOUPS AND SNACKS

Exmouth, A Cockle Woman 1906 53961

RECIPE

— · —

Crab Soup

225g/8oz fresh or frozen crab meat
50g/2oz butter
50g/2oz plain flour
900ml/1½ pints full cream milk
1.2 litres/2 pints chicken stock
Salt
White pepper
A good pinch of nutmeg
2 tablespoonfuls dry sherry
150ml/ ¼ pint double or whipping cream

Separate the white and dark crab meat. Melt the butter in a large pan, stir
in the flour and let it cook for one minute, then gradually add the milk,
stirring continually, and then the chicken stock. Add the dark crab meat,
salt, pepper and nutmeg and allow to simmer gently for about 15 minutes,
then add the white crab meat and the sherry. Raise the heat and bring
to just under boiling point, then reduce heat and simmer for a further 5
minutes. Check for seasoning and adjust if necessary.

The soup can be served as it is, or blend in a liquidizer or pass through a
sieve if a smoother constancy is preferred. Serve with a swirl of cream.

— · —

St Ives, Lifeboatmen 1906 56543

RECIPE

—·—

Likky Soup

'Likky' is a Devon name for leeks.

3 large leeks
1 onion
3 medium-sized potatoes
1 rasher of streaky bacon
25g/1oz butter
1.2 litres/2 pints chicken stock
A pinch of grated nutmeg
150ml/ ¼ pint cream
Salt and pepper
Fresh chopped parsley to garnish

Wash the leeks thoroughly and chop them, keeping as much of the green part as possible. Peel and slice the onion. Peel the potatoes and chop into small cubes. Remove the rind from the bacon rasher and cut into small pieces. Put the bacon pieces into a large saucepan, and heat until the fat runs. Add the butter, and when it has melted add the leeks and onion. Cook for a few minutes until the vegetables have softened, then add the potato cubes and mix well. Add the stock and a pinch of nutmeg and bring to the boil, then reduce the heat, cover the pan and simmer for 25-30 minutes until the vegetables are soft and cooked. Season with salt and pepper.

This soup can be served as it is, or liquidized in a blender or passed through a sieve if a smoother consistency is preferred. Serve with a swirl of cream and some chopped fresh parsley on top.

—·—

Barnstaple, High Street 1903 49620

Port Isaac, A Cornish Fisherman 1896 56186

Cornish Pasty

One of the West Country's most famous dishes is the Cornish Pasty, a pastry 'envelope' containing meat and vegetables. It is said to have originally been devised as a portable lunch for Cornwall's fishermen, farmworkers, clayworkers and tin and copper miners. The style of the crimp (where the two edges meet and are sealed) varies from one area to another. There are many traditional versions of pasty recipes, but usually people just used to add whatever was available. Cornish pasties should never be made with mince, but with good chuck steak cut by hand into tiny pieces, and all the fillings – including the meat – should be put into the pasty uncooked. The vegetables should be coarsely grated, so that they all cook at the same time.

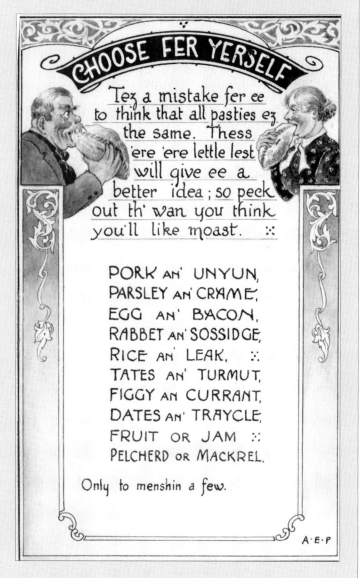

Frome, Cheap Street 1907 58850

RECIPE

Priddy Oggies

'Oggie' is a West Country name for pastry. Priddy Oggies, with a meat and cheese filling, were first served at the Miner's Arms at the village of Priddy in Somerset's Mendip Hills. They are unusual in that they are first baked in the oven and then deep-fried. This recipe makes 8 oggies.

For the pastry:
25g/1oz butter
25g/1oz lard
1 small egg yolk
Half a teaspoonful dry mustard
115g/4oz Cheddar cheese, grated
2½ tablespoonfuls of water
Pinch of salt
225g/8oz plain flour
600ml/1 pint vegetable oil, for deep frying

For the filling:
500g/1¼ lbs pork fillet
1 egg, beaten
75g/3oz mature Cheddar cheese, grated
2 tablespoonfuls chopped fresh parsley
Pinch of salt
Cayenne pepper
40g/1½ oz smoked bacon, cut into 8 strips

To make the pastry: mix all the ingredients except the flour in a warm bowl until they are soft. Cool the mixture in a refrigerator until it is firm, then sieve the flour and rub in the cooled mixture roughly. Divide the mixture into thirds. Take each piece and roll it 2 or 3 times into a 1cm (½ inch) slab, moistening the top of each slab slightly before laying them on top of each other. When finished, press down firmly and cut downwards into three pieces, repeating the rolling process twice more. Chill for 30 minutes.

To make the filling: trim the pork fillet and slice it lengthways into 2 pieces, then beat them gently until each piece is flat. Reserve half the beaten egg, then place the cheese, parsley, salt and cayenne pepper in the bowl with the rest of the egg and mix well. Spread the mixture evenly over the cut sides of the pork fillet, then roll up each piece, pressing down firmly. Chill for 30 minutes.To assemble the oggies: cut each roll of pork fillet into 4 slices and wrap a piece of bacon around each slice. Roll out the pastry and cut it into 8 equal squares. Lay a slice of the stuffed meat in the centre of each square of pastry, then moisten around the edges with a little water. Bring the pastry up and over the meat, pressing the edges together in a scalloped design. Press down the base slightly to flatten. Put the oggies on to a baking sheet, and brush each one with the remaining beaten egg.

Place the oggies in the centre of a pre-heated oven (200°C/400°F/Gas Mark 6) and bake for about 15 minutes, or until they are just starting to brown. Remove from the oven.

Heat the oil in a deep fryer to 180°C/350°F (or until a cube of brown bread browns in 30 seconds). Deep-fry the oggies until the pastry begins to brown, then drain them on paper towels and serve.

Porlock, High Street 1919 69270

Taunton, Fore Street 1902 48723x

RECIPE

~ · ~

Taunton Toast

4 thick slices of bead
50g/2oz butter or margarine
1 level tablespoonful dry English mustard
4 tablespoonfuls dry Somerset cider
225g/8oz grated strong Cheddar cheese
Salt and pepper to taste

Melt the butter in a saucepan over a gentle heat. Stir in the mustard, cider and cheese, and continue stirring until all the cheese has melted and the mixture is smooth and creamy. Season to taste. Toast the bread, then spread the cheese mixture on the slices. Place them under a hot grill until golden brown and bubbling.

~ · ~

Dialect Words from Somerset

'Addled' - gone off, rancid.

'Athirt' - across.

'Backalong' - some time ago.

'Bide' - stay.

'Cradlehood' - infancy.

'Crousty' - bad tempered.

'Dimpsey' - twilight, dusk.

'Dumbledore' - bumble bee.

'Muckers' - mates, friends.

'Right nottlin' - very cold.

'Ruckles' - peat stacks.

'Scrumping' - stealing apples.

'Scrumpy' - cider.

FISH

Brixham, The Harbour 1925 78490

RECIPE

—·—

Baked John Dory

Devon fish from both sea and rivers is famous, particularly its salmon, hake and sole, as well as shellfish, scallops and crab, but a wide variety of fish is caught. One of the most popular fish caught from the famous fishing port of Brixham is John Dory, often known as St Peter's fish – the black 'thumbprints' on each side of its head are said to be the marks of St Peter, who was a fisherman.

4 John Dory fillets
225g/8oz prawns
50g/2oz button mushrooms
1 teaspoonful anchovy essence
1 egg, beaten (optional)
Salt and pepper
1 tablespoonful white wine or cider

Pre-heat the oven to 220°C/400°F/Gas Mark 6.

Wash the fish and wipe it dry. Cut it into oblong strips. Finely chop the prawns and mushrooms, combine in a bowl and add the anchovy essence. Moisten, if necessary, with a little beaten egg. Put a little of this mixture on to each strip of fish and roll up into little parcels. Put into a buttered ovenproof dish, season with salt and pepper and moisten with the white wine or cider. Cover with buttered greaseproof paper and cook in the pre-heated oven for about 15 minutes, depending on the thickness of the fillets.

—·—

Pilchards

Cornwall is encircled by water, surrounded by the sea on three sides and separated from the rest of England by the River Tamar. Not surprisingly, the sea has always provided both a living and a staple food for the people of Cornwall. Cornish fishermen netted every fish they could, but the pilchard was the most crucial and sought after (pilchards are full-grown specimens of sardines). The pilchard trade was seasonal, and in July the waters of Mounts Bay, extending in a broad sweep from the Lizard in the east to Land's End in the west, were busy with boats competing for a share in the catch. The lives of whole communities revolved around catching and processing the fish – gutting, barrelling, salting and delivering. Later in the year the boats pursued herring, followed by mackerel in the spring.

Mousehole, The Harbour 1927 79945

RECIPE

— • —

Stargazy Pie

One of Cornwall's most famous traditional recipes is that for Stargazy Pie, in which pilchards are placed in a pie dish with their heads resting on the rim. Other ingredients such as herbs and bacon are added, and the fish are then covered with pastry, leaving the heads outside the pie, 'gazing at the stars'. The dish is traditionally linked with the village of Mousehole, where it is eaten on 23rd December – Tom Bawcock's Eve.

The story goes that many years ago, during a long period of bad weather, the Mousehole fishing fleet was unable to leave the harbour, and the village was starving. One brave man, Tom Bawcock, was so concerned that he managed to put to sea and catch just enough fish to feed the village. The fish (some stories say there were seven varieties) were made into a pie with their heads left on, so that nothing would be wasted. Several varieties of fish can be used, such as small mackerel, herrings or pilchards, but pilchards (or fresh sardines, as they are now known) are particularly authentic.

> 6-8 fish, gutted, cleaned and boned, but with the heads and tails left on
> 2 eggs
> 3 rashers of bacon, chopped into squares
> Grated zest and juice of 1 lemon
> 1 onion, finely chopped
> Seasoning – salt, pepper and tarragon to taste
> 500g/1 lb shortcrust or flaky pastry

Grate the zest from the lemon, and reserve. Cut 2 slices of lemon for decoration, then squeeze the juice and reserve. Boil the eggs until soft (not very hard boiled), and cut into small pieces.

Roll out half the pastry and line the bottom of a 20cm (8 inch) pie dish. Arrange the pilchards in the pie dish like the spokes of a wheel, leaving the heads on the rim. Fill the gaps between the fish with the mixture of chopped onion, bacon, eggs and seasoning. Pour over the lemon juice and zest. Cover the pie with the other half of the pastry, pressing down well between the heads of the fish to seal, leaving the fish heads outside the lid. Brush the pastry lid with beaten egg or milk to give a nice glaze. Cook the pie in the middle of a pre-heated oven (200°C/400°F/Gas Mark 6) for about 30 minutes, until the pastry is crisp and golden.

— • —

St Ives, The Harbour, Cleaning the Fish 1925 78658

RECITE

— · —

Stuffed Mackerel with Gooseberry Sauce

Gooseberries have long been a favourite accompaniment to mackerel in many parts of England, although in the Bristol area a rhubarb sauce is traditional with this fish.

4 mackerel, gutted and de-scaled
1 tablespoonful chopped parsley
1 tablespoonful chopped thyme
Half a teaspoonful grated lemon rind
1 tablespoonful lemon juice
25g/1oz soft white breadcrumbs
Seasoned flour
225g/8oz gooseberries
Sugar to taste

Pre-heat the oven to 180°C/350°F/Gas Mark 4.

Wash and dry the mackerel, and clean them. Mix the parsley, thyme, lemon rind, lemon juice and soft breadcrumbs and stuff the mackerel with this mixture. Roll the fish lightly in seasoned flour. Melt a little butter or oil in a baking pan and, when it is very hot, put in the mackerel. Put into the pre-heated oven and bake for 25 minutes, carefully turning the fish over halfway through.

Meanwhile, for the gooseberry sauce, simmer the gooseberries in very little water until they are soft. Rub them through a sieve and sweeten lightly. Warm the gooseberry sauce through before serving with the mackerel.

— · —

'Great Drake, whose shippe aboute the world's wide wast
In three years did a golden girdle cast.
Who with fresh streames refresht this Towne that first
Though kist with waters, yet did pire for thirst.'

Plymouth, Drake's Statue 1930 83293

Plymouth, Bedford Street 1904   52407

RECIPE

— · —

Trout with Almonds and Cream

Drake's Leat, Plymouth's original water supply, was built by Sir Francis Drake in 1590-91 at a cost of £300. The leat brought water seventeen miles from the head of the River Meavy, 'carried every way to get the vantage of the hills'. The distance as the crow flies is only nine miles, and the leat represents a fair engineering achievement.

For the last 400 years, the bringing of fresh, clean water to Plymouth by Drake has been celebrated by the annual 'Fyshinge Feaste' in June. The Mayor of Plymouth and his council congregate at the head weir of the leat, where official toasts are drunk, from a goblet filled with water from the leat, 'to the pious memory of Sir Francis Drake'. Another goblet, this time filled with red wine, is then passed round, with each person drinking a further toast: 'May the descendants of him who brought us water never want'. As part of the tradition, a meal of local trout caught from the leat is then eaten.

    4 trout, gutted and cleaned
    Flour for coating the fish
    Salt and pepper
    175g/6oz butter
    50g/2oz blanched almonds
    Juice of half a lemon
    150ml/ ¼ pint single cream

Mix the flour with salt and pepper and use to coat the fish on both sides. Melt 115g/4oz of the butter in a frying pan. Slide in the trout and cook for 15 minutes, turning halfway through cooking time, until they are golden brown on both sides and cooked through. Drain the trout and keep warm on a serving dish.

Clean the pan, then melt the remaining butter in it. Add the almonds and fry carefully until they are lightly browned. Stir in the lemon juice. Heat the cream gently in a separate pan and pour over the fish. Sprinkle with the almonds and serve.

— · —

Paignton, Bathing Beach 1896 38545

RECIPE

— · —

Tamar Salmon in Pastry

The River Exe is Devon's main river. It rises in north Devon, on Exmoor, and flows south for almost 50 miles before reaching the sea at Exmouth. In 1924 a salmon weighing 64lb was caught in the River Exe by fisherman Richard Voysey. Further west, excellent salmon is also caught in the River Tamar, which forms much of the border between Devon and Cornwall.

900g/2 lbs fillet of salmon
Salt and pepper
Lemon juice
1 tablespoonful olive oil
675g/1½ lbs puff pastry
225g/8oz onions or shallots
Half a teaspoonful chopped tarragon
115g/4oz button mushrooms
1 egg, beaten, for glazing the pastry

Oven temperature: 190°C/375°F/Gas Mark 5.

Season the salmon with salt, pepper and lemon juice. Heat the olive oil in a large frying pan and lightly fry the salmon on both sides. Take the salmon out of the pan and leave to cool. Roll out the puff pastry on a floured surface to form an oblong shape large enough to enclose the salmon. Chop the onions or shallots very finely, and sweat them in the pan the fish was cooked in, together with the tarragon. Allow to cool, then spread over one half of the pastry. Thinly slice the mushrooms and place them on top of the onions. Season with salt and pepper. Place the salmon on top of the vegetables, fold over the other half of the pastry to enclose it all, and seal the edges. Place, folded side down, on a well-greased baking sheet and brush the top with beaten egg to glaze. Bake in the pre-heated oven for 1 hour, until the pastry is crisp and golden brown.

— · —

Saltash, The Royal Albert Bridge and the River Tamar 1890 22477

MEAT AND GAME

Winsford c1960 W112018

RECIPE

Somerset Pork with Apples

25g/1oz butter
500g/1¼ lbs pork loin, cut into small pieces
12 baby onions or shallots, peeled and left whole
2 teaspoonfuls grated lemon rind
300ml/ ½ pint dry cider
150ml/ ½ pint stock
2 crisp eating apples, cored and sliced but not peeled
3 tablespoonfuls chopped fresh parsley
100ml/3½ fl oz whipping cream
Salt and pepper

Heat the butter in a large sauté or frying pan, and brown the pork in batches. Transfer the pork to a bowl. Add the onions to the pan and cook gently until they are soft. Stir in the lemon rind, cider and stock, increase heat and boil for a few minutes. Return the pork to the pan, reduce heat and cook gently for 25-30 minutes, until the meat is tender. Add the apples to the pan and cook for a further 5 minutes.

Use a slotted spoon to transfer the pork, apples and onions to a warmed serving dish, and keep warm. Stir the cream and parsley into the cooking pan, and allow the sauce to bubble so that it thickens slightly. Season to taste, then pour over the pork and serve whilst it is hot.

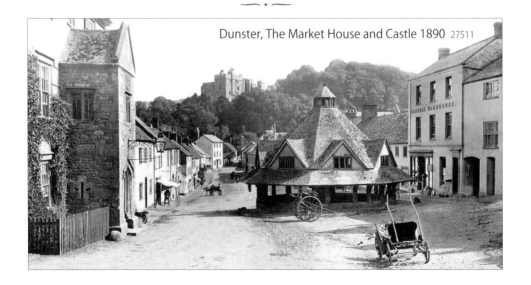

Dunster, The Market House and Castle 1890 27511

Exeter, Guildhall 1896 38003

RECIPE

~·~

Exeter Beef Stew and Parsley Dumplings

Parsley dumplings are traditionally served with Exeter Stew. In south Devon, dumplings are called 'Nackerjacks', in north Devon they are known as 'Naggerjacks', and in Somerset they are known as 'doughboys'.

450g/1 lb stewing steak
25g/1oz lard
1 onion
2 carrots
1 small turnip
400ml/ ¾ pint stock
25g/1oz flour
Salt and pepper

Cut the meat into cubes and toss them in seasoned flour so that all sides are coated. Melt the lard in a large saucepan. Peel and slice the onion and cook it in the lard until it is soft and transparent. Add the meat and cook until the cubes are browned on all sides. Pour in the stock and bring to the boil. Peel the turnip and cut it into small chunks, peel and slice the carrots, and add to the saucepan. Add seasoning. Reduce heat, cover the pan and simmer the stew gently for 2-2½ hours, until the meat is very tender. Add the parsley dumplings (recipe below) for the last 20-25 minutes of cooking time.

Parsley Dumplings

115g/4oz fresh white breadcrumbs
50g/2oz shredded suet
A pinch of salt and pepper
1 tablespoonful chopped parsley
1 egg

Mix together the breadcrumbs, suet, salt and pepper and chopped parsley. Lightly beat the egg and mix it into the mixture to bind it all together. Drop spoonfuls of the dumpling mixture into the stew for the last 20-25 minutes of the cooking time.

~·~

Dialect Words from Dorset

'Ballyrag' - to scold.

'Bibber' - to shiver with cold.

'Blather' - an uproar, a noise, a fuss.

'Chippols' - young onions.

'Clavy' - the mantelpiece.

'Culver' - a wood pigeon.

'Dabster' - an expert.

'Limber' - slender.

'Maggotty' - fanciful.

'Rafty' - rancid.

'Tinklebobs' - icicles.

'Quilkin' - a frog.

'Yaffle' - a green woodpecker.

Lyme Regis, Victoria Pier 1912 65043

RECITE

Dorset Rabbit

1 jointed rabbit
25g/1oz flour
Salt and freshly ground black pepper
115g/4oz streaky bacon rashers
150ml/ ¼ pint dry cider

For the topping:
115g/4oz shredded suet
225g/8oz fresh breadcrumbs
2 onions, peeled and chopped very fine
Grated rind of half a lemon
1 teaspoonful dried sage
1 beaten egg
A little milk

Blanch the rabbit joints in boiling water, then pat dry. Season the flour with salt and pepper. Roll the rabbit joints in the seasoned flour so that they are coated all over, then place them in a casserole dish. Lay the bacon rashers on top of the rabbit joints, and pour the cider over.

Mix together the suet, breadcrumbs, grated lemon rind, dried sage and finely chopped onions. Bind the mixture together with the beaten egg and a little milk.

Cover the rabbit with the topping. Cover the casserole with its lid and bake for two hours in a moderate oven, 180°C/350°F/Gas Mark 4, then remove the lid and cook for a further 20-25 minutes, so that the topping browns.

Maiden Newton, Dorchester Road 1906 54563

RECIPE

— · —

Pheasant with Mushrooms

1 pheasant, jointed
250ml/8 fl oz red wine
3 tablespoonfuls of oil
4 tablespoonfuls of sherry vinegar
1 onion, peeled and chopped
2 rashers of smoked bacon, cut into strips
350g/12oz chestnut mushrooms, sliced
350ml/12 fl oz chicken stock
1 bouquet garni
Salt and pepper

Place the pheasant in a shallow dish, add the wine, half the oil and half the vinegar, and scatter half the chopped onions over the joints. Season, then cover and leave in a cool place to marinade for 8-12 hours, turning the joints from time to time so that they infuse the flavours.

Pre-heat the oven to 160°C/325°C/Gas Mark 3.

Take the pheasant joints from the dish and pat them dry with kitchen paper, and reserve the marinade. Heat the remaining oil in a large casserole dish, and brown the joints, then transfer them to a plate. Add the bacon and remaining onion to the casserole, and cook gently until the onion is soft. Add the mushrooms and continue to cook for a further 3 minutes. Stir in the remaining vinegar, and boil until it has reduced. Add the reserved marinade, the stock and the bouquet garni and cook for a few minutes. Return the pheasant joints to the casserole, put on the lid and cook in the pre-heated oven for about 1½ hours.

When the joints are cooked, transfer them to a serving dish and keep warm. Boil the cooking juice left in the casserole dish until it has reduced and thickened slightly. Remove the bouquet garni, pour the juice over the pheasant and serve.

— · —

Lynmouth, Countisbury Hill, The Blue Ball Inn 1907 59405x

Lynmouth, Cherry Bridge 1907 59424

RECIPE

～ · ～

Exmoor Lamb Stew

4 lamb chops
25g/1oz butter
450g/1 lb small potatoes
115g/4oz mushrooms
50g/2oz button onions or shallots
150ml/ ¼ pint stock
4 tablespoonfuls white wine
4 tablespoonfuls cream
Salt and pepper
Fresh herbs, such as parsley, thyme, lovage,
    finely chopped

Melt the butter in a large saucepan and fry the lamb chops on both sides until browned. Remove the chops from the pan, and put in the potatoes, mushrooms and onions. Cook the vegetables for 5 minutes, then remove them from the pan.

Drain any fat from the pan, and add the stock, wine and cream, stirring thoroughly to blend it all together. Return the lamb chops and the vegetables to the pan, together with the finely chopped fresh herbs, and season with salt and pepper.

Cover the pan with its lid and simmer the stew gently for about 1 hour, until the lamb chops are tender.

～ · ～

RECIPE

~ . ~

Devonshire Squab Pie

Squabs are young pigeons, which is what this pie was originally made with, although nowadays it is more usual to use lamb.

675g/1½ lbs lamb neck fillets, cut into 12 pieces
1 onion, thinly sliced
350g/12oz leeks, sliced
1 large cooking apple, peeled, cored and diced
Half a teaspoonful of ground allspice
Half a teaspoonful of freshly grated nutmeg
150ml/¼ pint lamb, beef or vegetable stock
225g/8oz shortcrust pastry
Beaten egg or milk to glaze
Salt and pepper

Pre-heat the oven to 200°C/400°F/Gas Mark 6.

Layer the meat, onion, leek and apple in a pie dish, sprinkling in the spices and seasoning as you go, to taste. Pour in the stock.

Roll out the pastry to 2cm (¾ inch) larger than the top of the pie dish. Cut a narrow strip from around the pastry, fit it around the dampened rim of the dish, then brush with water. Lay the pastry over the dish, and press the edges together to seal them. Brush the pastry lid with beaten egg or milk, and make a hole in the centre.

Bake the pie in the pre-heated oven for 20 minutes, then reduce the oven temperature to 180° C/350°F/ Gas Mark 4 and continue to cook for 1-1¼ hours, covering the pie with foil if the pastry begins to brown too much.

~ . ~

RECIPE

— · —

Dorset Sausage

This is like a coarse terrine, and is eaten cold, in slices – ideal for a picnic.

450g/1 lb minced beef
450g/1 lb minced ham
225g/8oz fresh breadcrumbs
A pinch of freshly grated nutmeg
Half a teaspoonful ground mace
3 eggs, beaten
Salt and pepper

Mix the meats together, then add the breadcrumbs and mix again. Mix in the eggs and seasonings.

Grease a 900g (2 lb) loaf tin, and fill with the mixture. Cover the tin with foil and stand it in a roasting tin filled with enough very hot water to come halfway up its sides. Bake in a moderate oven (180°C/350°C/Gas Mark 4) for 1½ - 2 hours, topping up the tin with more hot water if necessary.

Leave to cool completely before turning out.

— · —

Swindon, Men Leaving The Great Western Railway Works 1913 S254607

Dialect Words from Wiltshire

'Cack handed' - left handed, or clumsy.

'Chuckypigs', **'chuggypigs'** or **'grampfywigs'** - woodlice.

'Emmet' - an ant.

'Gally-bagger', or **'gally-crow'** - a scarecrow.

'Gert' - big, large.

'Loppity' - feeling ill, run-down, under the weather.

'Nammet' - the mid-day snack.

'Narration' - a fuss, or commotion.

'Shrammed'- chilled to the bone.

'Spadgers' - sparrows.

'Teg' - a sheep, thus 'tegman' - shepherd.

Bishopstone, Post Office and Stores 1908 B298001

RECIPE

~ . ~

Wiltshire Market Day Dinner

6 pork chops
2 pigs' kidneys, sliced
450g/1 lb onions, peeled and sliced
1 apple
1 teaspoonful chopped sage
Salt and pepper
450g/1 lb potatoes

Put the chops into an ovenproof casserole. Cover with the sliced kidneys and onions. Peel, core and slice the apple and put on top. Sprinkle on the sage, and season well with salt and pepper. Peel and slice the potatoes and cover the top of the dish with them. Pour on 150ml/¼ pint water or stock, cover and cook at 170°C/325°F/Gas Mark 3 for about three hours.

~ . ~

Wootton Bassett, The Market, High Street 1906 W171507

CHEESE AND VEGETABLE DISHES

~ . ~

RECIPE

~ . ~

Candied Sweet Potatoes

Sir Walter Raleigh is famous for introducing the ordinary potato to England from the New World, but Plymouth's Sir Francis Drake and Sir John Hawkins brought sweet potatoes to England around 1563-65. Drake said of sweet potatoes: 'These potatoes be the most delicate rootes that may be eaten, and doe farre exceed out passeneps or carets. Their pines be of the bignes of two fists, the outside whereof is of the making of a pine-apple, but it is soft like the rinde of a cucomber, and the inside eateth like an apple but it is more delicious than any sweet apple sugared.' Sweet potatoes are now easily available in most supermarkets and greengrocer shops, and can be cooked in all the ways that ordinary potatoes are used, but cook much more quickly. This recipe for candied sweet potatoes is a dish traditionally served at Thanksgiving in the USA.

800g/1 lb 10oz orange sweet potatoes
75g/3oz butter, melted
115g/4oz soft brown sugar
2 teaspoonfuls grated lemon zest
1 tablespoonful lemon juice
125ml/4 fl oz orange juice
1 cinnamon stick

Pre-heat the oven to 180°C/350°F/Gas Mark 4.

Peel the sweet potatoes and cut them into thick rounds. Arrange the rounds in a greased ovenproof dish, and pour the melted butter over the top. Add the sugar, lemon and orange juices and the cinnamon stick. Cover the dish with its lid or a piece of foil, and bake in the pre-heated oven for about 30 minutes. Uncover, and stir the mixture gently, remove the cinnamon stick and sprinkle the lemon zest over the top. Cook, uncovered, for a further 20-30 minutes, until the top is slightly crisp.

~ . ~

RECIPE

Gloucester Cheese Stew

In former times, the milk of different breeds of cow was used to make different cheeses, and traditionally the Old Gloucester breed was considered the only cow for making Double Gloucester cheese.

450g/1 lb potatoes
275ml/ ½ pint milk
Salt and freshly ground black pepper
3 onions
225g/ ½ lb Double Gloucester cheese, grated

Peel the potatoes, cut them into thin slices and place in a saucepan with the milk. Season with salt and pepper, then simmer them gently until almost tender (10-15 minutes). Take the potato slices out of the pan, and reserve the milk. Peel the onions and chop them finely. Grease a medium-sized casserole or ovenproof dish. Put layers of potato, onion and cheese into the dish, seasoning each layer, finishing with a layer of cheese. Pour over the milk that the potatoes were cooked in. Bake the dish, uncovered, for one hour in a medium oven – 180°C/350°F/Gas Mark 4 – until the top is golden brown.

Birdlip, Village Life 1907 59061x

RECIPE

— · —

Cabbage and Potato Pie

Cabbages are said to be have been introduced to England by Sir Anthony Ashley, who imported cabbages from Holland in the 16th century to grow in the kitchen garden of his house at Wimborne St Giles in Dorset.

> 450g/1 lb potatoes
> 450g/1 lb cabbage
> 2 onions, peeled and thinly sliced
> 25g/1oz butter
> A little milk
> A pinch of salt
> Freshly ground black pepper
> 115g/4oz cheese, grated

Oven temperature: 190°C/375°F/Gas Mark 5.

Boil the potatoes until they are very soft, then mash them with butter and a little milk. Season with salt and pepper. Boil or steam the cabbage until it is tender. Mix together the mashed potato, cabbage and onion slices, and turn into a greased pie dish. Sprinkle the grated cheese on to the top of the pie, and bake in a pre-heated oven for 20-30 minutes, until the top has browned.

— · —

Turnip

The town of Marazion in Cornwall was known in Victorian times for its cultivation of a particularly delicious species of turnip.

St Ives, On the Beach 1890 24178

Anyone for Nettles?

The young shoots of nettles have been eaten in the spring by country people for centuries, as a welcome source of fresh greens at the time of year before other vegetables are ready to eat. Only the tender top sprigs should be eaten, and can be cooked in the same way as spinach, or made into a tasty soup with pieces of bacon and milk. The acid which causes the nettles to sting is destroyed by cooking. The tradition of eating nettles in Dorset is continued in one of England's most eccentric events, the annual Stinging Nettle Eating Challenge which is held at the Bottle Inn at Marshwood, in west Dorset – the brave competitors who take part actually eat raw nettles!

Weymouth, The Sands 1909 61597

Onion Sellers

For many years Plymouth, with its direct ferry service to Brittany, saw French onion sellers in the town every year. This photograph shows two young lads standing by the harbour wall with their strings of onions. With their grimy jackets and trousers, they give every impression of having endured an uncomfortable passage.

Plymouth, Onion Sellers 1907 59208

RECIPE

~ . ~

Somerset Cheese Bake

350g/12oz Cheddar cheese, grated
4 large onions, peeled and finely sliced
Salt and pepper
175g/6oz wholemeal breadcrumbs
6 tablespoonfuls of milk
25g/1oz butter

Pre-heat the oven to 180°C/350°F/Gas Mark 4.

Put a layer of cheese, then a layer of onion, and then a layer of breadcrumbs
in a shallow ovenproof dish, reserving a little of the cheese and breadcrumbs,
and seasoning each layer to taste. Pour on the milk, and finish with a layer of
cheese topped with the remaining breadcrumbs, and sprinkle the top with the
remaining cheese. Dot the top with small pieces of butter. Bake in the pre-heated
oven for 35-40 minutes, until the onion is cooked and the top is crisp and brown.

~ . ~

Clevedon, The Pier 1892 31251

Cheddar Cheese

Cheddar is a small town to the south of the Mendip Hills in Somerset, close to the spectacular Cheddar Gorge, which has given its name to a cheese that has now become world famous. Originally, the cheese had to be produced within 30 miles of Wells Cathedral to be classed as 'Cheddar cheese'. This type of cheese has become so popular that is now made all over the world, but there are still a few farms in Somerset where 'true' Cheddar cheese is made.

The biggest recorded Cheddar cheese ever made was produced for Queen Victoria's wedding in 1840; it weighed 11 cwt and used the milk from 737 cows. The monster cheese was made by the farmers of the villages of East and West Pennard, near Glastonbury in Somerset, as a wedding present for the royal couple.

Cheddar, The Village c1873 6982

The old lady in this photograph has been identified as Sally Spencer. She made her living by collecting and selling to visitors fragments of spar chipped from the sides of Cheddar Gorge in Somerset. The hills above the village are rich in flowers that peep out from rock fissures into the sunlight, and Sally also found a ready market for the local flowers known as Cheddar Pinks. By Sally Spencer's time Cheddar's famous Gorge and caves had caused the village to become quite a tourist spot, and she must have been grateful to the crowds of tourists for providing her with a regular income.

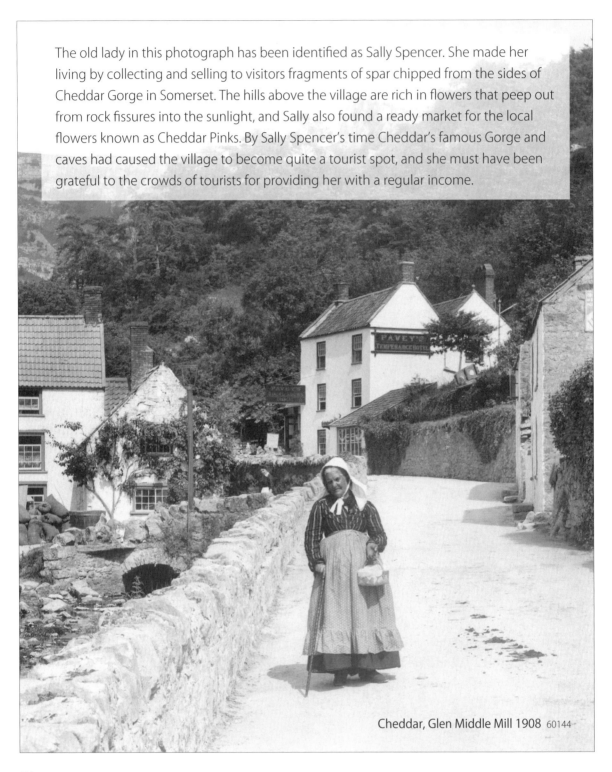

Cheddar, Glen Middle Mill 1908 60144

Shepton Mallet, A Shop in Town Street 1899 44843x

PUDDINGS AND DESSERTS

Exeter, Stepcote Hill 1911 63678

RECITE

— · —

Exeter Pudding

Mrs Beeton included a recipe for Exeter Pudding in her 'Book of Household Management'.

> 275g/10oz of breadcrumbs
> 115g/4oz of sago
> 200g/7oz of finely-chopped suet
> 175g/6oz of moist sugar
> The rind of half a lemon
> 150ml/ ¼ pint of rum
> 7 eggs
> 4 tablespoonfuls of cream
> 4 small sponge cakes
> 50g/2 oz of ratafia biscuits
> 225g/8oz of jam (or a small-size jar)

'Put the breadcrumbs into a basin with the sago, suet, sugar, minced lemon-peel, rum and 4 eggs; stir these ingredients well together, then add 3 more eggs and the cream, and let the mixture be well beaten. Then butter a mould, strew in a few breadcrumbs, and cover the bottom with a layer of ratafias; then put in a layer of the mixture, then a layer of sliced sponge cake spread thickly with any kind of jam; then add some ratafias, then some of the mixture and sponge cake, and so on until the mould is full, taking care that a layer of the mixture is on the top of the pudding. Bake in a good oven from three-quarter to 1 hour, and serve with the following sauce:
Put 3 tablespoonfuls of black-currant jelly into a stewpan, add 2 glasses of sherry, and, when warm, turn the pudding out of the mould, pour the sauce over it, and serve hot.'

— · —

RECIPE

— · —

Bath Ground Rice Pudding

225g/8oz shortcrust pastry

50g/2oz ground rice

25g/1oz sugar

275ml/ ½ pint single cream

275ml/ ½ pint milk

2 eggs

25g/1oz butter

1 teaspoonful sherry, or a few drops of vanilla essence if preferred

Freshly grated nutmeg

Line a 20cm (8in) flan tin with the shortcrust pastry and bake blind at 190°C/375°F/Gas Mark 5 for 15 minutes.

Put the milk and cream into a saucepan, sprinkle in the ground rice and sugar, and cook in a double boiler (stand the pan inside a larger pan half filled with boiling water, over heat), whisking all the time to prevent lumps forming. Simmer for 5 minutes, and remove from the heat when thickened.

Cool the mixture, then beat in the eggs, butter and sherry or vanilla. Fill the pastry case with the mixture and bake at 160°C/325°F/Gas Mark 3 for about 30 minutes. Grate some fresh nutmeg over the top before serving.

— · —

RECIPE

— . —

Apple Dumplings

4 large cooking apples
4 teaspoonfuls mincemeat
4 teaspoonfuls soft brown sugar
Half a teaspoonful cinnamon
225g/8oz shortcrust pastry
Milk to glaze
Caster sugar

Pre-heat the oven to 180°C/350°F/Gas Mark 4.

Peel and core the apples. Stuff the cavity of each apple with a teaspoonful of mincemeat and a teaspoonful of brown sugar. Sprinkle the cinnamon over each apple.

Divide the pastry into four equal pieces. Roll each one out into a square big enough to wrap around an apple. Place one apple in the centre of each square, dampen the edges with water, and fold up the corners to meet at the top like a parcel, and enclose the apple.

Place the dumplings in an ovenproof dish and brush with milk to glaze. Sprinkle with caster sugar. Bake in the pre-heated oven for about half an hour – test to see if ready to serve by sticking a skewer into a dumpling to make sure the apple is soft. Serve with cream or custard.

— . —

A Taste of the SOUTH-WEST

Salisbury, Poultry Cross and Silver Street 1906 56359

PUDDINGS AND DESSERTS

RECITE

— . —

Moonshine

This recipe recalls the nickname of 'Moonrakers' which was given to Wiltshire folk. The story goes that on the night of a full moon, some Bishops Cannings men were busily transporting smuggled kegs of brandy in a wagon-load of hay when they heard the sound of approaching excise men. Quick as they could, they extracted the kegs and threw them into a nearby pond. The excise men were put off, but not fooled – they left, but doubled back to discover the smugglers attempting to recover the submerged kegs with hay rakes. When asked what they were doing, the smugglers indicated the clear reflection of the moon and uttered something like 'Zomebody 'ave lost thic thur cheese and we'm a-rakin for un in thic thur pond.' The excise men smiled at the simpletons and left. The moonrakers smiled at the simpletons and did the same – whilst enjoying the brandy.

> 50g/2oz butter
> 6 thin slices of white bread, with the crusts removed
> 50g/2oz sultanas
> 50g/2oz caster sugar
> 400ml/ ¾ pint milk
> 150ml/ ¼ pint single cream
> 3 eggs
> Grated rind of half a lemon
> Freshly grated nutmeg

Oven temperature: 180°C/350°F/Gas Mark 4.

Use some of the butter to grease a shallow ovenproof dish. Use the rest of the butter to spread on the bread slices. Cut the bread into strips and arrange in layers in the dish, buttered side up, sprinkling each layer with sultanas and sugar, finishing with a layer of buttered bread.

Break the eggs into a bowl and beat. Heat the milk and cream to just below boiling point, then pour it onto the eggs, stirring all the time. Add the lemon rind. Pour the mixture over the bread in the dish, sprinkle the top with grated nutmeg. Allow to stand for 30 minutes, then bake in the pre-heated oven for 35-40 minutes, until the custard is set and the top is crisp.

— . —

RECIPE

—·—

Plum and Walnut Crumble

The long estuaries of the rivers of south Devon – which are actually river valleys formed when the sea level rose at the end of the last Ice Age – are very sheltered; as a result they have their own microclimates, which allow market gardening and fruit growing to flourish. Dittisham, on the Dart, was once well-known for its plum orchards.

> 75g/3oz walnut pieces
> 75g/3oz butter or margarine, diced
> 175g/6oz plain flour
> 175g/6oz demerara sugar
> 1kg/2 lbs plums, halved and stoned

Pre-heat the oven to 180°C/350°F/Gas Mark 4.

Spread the nuts on a baking sheet and place in the oven for 8-10 minutes, until they are evenly coloured.

Butter a 1.2 litre (2 pint) baking dish. Put the plums into the dish and stir in the nuts and half the demerara sugar. Rub the butter or margarine into the flour until the mixture resembles coarse crumbs. Stir in the remaining sugar and continue to rub in until fine crumbs are formed. Cover the fruit with the crumb mixture and press it down lightly. Bake the pudding in the pre-heated oven for about 45 minutes, until the top is golden brown and the fruit tender. Serve with custard or cream.

—·—

RECIPE

— · —

Figgy Hobbin

Figgy Hobbin (or Figgy 'Obbin) is a traditional recipe from Cornwall. It also known as Figgy Duff. 'Figs' is the name used in Cornwall for raisins, although currants can also be used.

> 225g/8oz plain flour
> 1 teaspoonful baking powder
> A pinch of salt
> 115g/4oz suet
> 75g/3oz raisins (or currants, if used)
> Grated peel of half a lemon
> Cold water to mix
> A little milk for glazing

Pre-heat the oven to 180°C/350°C/Gas Mark 4.

Mix together the flour, baking powder, suet and salt, and add enough cold water to form a stiff dough. Roll out the dough on a floured surface to about 1cm (half an inch) thick, and sprinkle the raisins (or currants) and lemon peel over it. Roll up the pastry to make a cake like a Swiss roll, then pinch and seal the ends. Make a criss-cross pattern on the top with a sharp knife, and brush with milk. Bake in the pre-heated oven for about 30 minutes, and serve hot.

— · —

Dialect Words from Cornwall

'Aglets' - Hawthorn berries.

'Bulhorns' - snails.

'Cakey' - soft, feeble minded.

'Emmets' or **'murrians'** - ants – nowadays both words are also used for tourists.

'Flam-new' - brand new.

'Grammersow' - a woodlouse.

'Knockers' - Spirits that dwell underground, especially in mines.

'Steeved' - very cold, frozen through.

'Teasy' - bad-tempered.

'Urts' - whortleberries, or bilberries.

Launceston, People in Fore Street 1893 32166x

TEATIME AND BAKING

Eype, Jessamine Cottage 1897 40089

RECIPE

Dorset Apple Cake

225g/8oz self-raising flour
115g/4oz butter or margarine
A pinch of salt
450g/1 lb apples
115g/4oz caster sugar
1 egg
1-2 tablespoonfuls milk
50g/2oz currants or raisins
A pinch of cinnamon or mixed spice, whichever is preferred
Demerara sugar to sprinkle on top

Pre-heat the oven to 180°C/350°F/Gas Mark 4.

Sift the flour and salt into a bowl. Rub in the butter or margarine until the mixture resembles breadcrumbs. Peel, core and chop the apples into small pieces and add to the mixture, and then add the dried fruit, sugar and cinnamon or mixed spice.

Beat the egg with the milk, and add to the mixture. Mix it all together well, forming a firm dough, and place it in a greased 20cm (8 inch) round cake tin. Sprinkle the top with demerara sugar, and bake in the pre-heated oven for about 1 hour.

This can be eaten either cold or hot, with the slices split open and spread with butter. It also makes a delicious pudding, served hot with cream, custard or ice-cream.

RECIPE

—.—

Bath Buns

Bath Buns were originally topped with 'confits', caraway seeds that had been dipped into boiling sugar, but this flavour is not to modern tastes and a crushed sugar topping is used instead. Bath buns were a great favourite of Jane Austen when she lived in the city.

> 15g/ ½ oz fresh yeast, or 10g/ ¼ oz dried yeast
> 1 teaspoonful salt
> 300ml/ ½ pint tepid milk
> 350g/12oz plain flour
> 115g/4oz butter
> 75g/3oz caster sugar
> 2 eggs, beaten
> 50g/2oz candied peel, chopped
> 50g/2oz crushed limp sugar

Cream the yeast with the sugar and add to the tepid milk. (If using dried yeast, mix with the sugar and half the milk. Leave in a warm place until frothy, then add the rest of the milk.) Put the flour in a bowl and pour the yeast mixture into a well in the middle. Leave until frothy.

Cream the butter and sugar, add the egg, reserving a little to glaze, and work into the dough. Reserve a little peel for decoration, then add the rest to the dough. Cover the dough with a cloth and leave in a warm place to rise for about 40 minutes.

Turn out and knead, then shape into small buns and place on a greased baking sheet, well spaced out. Leave to rise for a further 15-20 minutes, then brush with the rest of the egg, sprinkle with the coarsely crushed sugar and a little chopped peel. Bake in a pre-heated oven for about 30 minutes, 180°C/350°F/Gas Mark 4.

—.—

Bath, Great Pultenay Street 1890 25130

Bath Buns, and Oliver Biscuits

The popularity of Bath increased dramatically in the mid 18th century after Dr William Oliver, an authority on gout, opened the Royal Mineral Water Hospital offering treatments for that complaint. Dr Oliver's other claims to fame are that he devised the recipe for Bath Buns, and also that he invented the Bath Oliver biscuit; he was an anti-obesity campaigner and these lightweight biscuits were an early slimming aid. It is said that Dr Oliver left the recipe to his coachman, Atkins, after his death, with the sum of £100 and a large quantity of flour. Atkins opened a shop in Green Street to sell the biscuits, and became a rich man. The business later passed to a Mr Norris, who sold out to a baker called Carter. After two further changes of ownership, the Bath Oliver biscuit recipe passed to James Fortt in the 1950s. In 1952 over 80,000 biscuits a day were being made in Bath, but although they are still available, they are no longer made in the city.

RECIPE

— . —

Sally Lunn Cake

The oldest house in Bath can be found at 4 North Parade Passage. The building currently houses Sally Lunn's tearooms and museum, traditionally supposed to be named after a French Huguenot refugee called Sally Lunn (her real name was probably Solange Luyon), who moved into the house in 1680 and became famous for baking her version of yeast-based teacakes. However, there are many other interpretations of the origin of the famous 'Sally Lunn Cakes'; one says that Sally was the daughter of a pastry cook in Bath, and another that there was actually no one named Sally at all, and the name of the cakes comes from an old street cry in corrupted French, 'Solet lune', for 'sol et lune', the French words for sun and moon, which may have been used to describe the golden-topped buns.

For the yeast batter:	For the dough:	For the glaze:
75g/3oz plain flour	175g/6oz plain flour	1 tablespoonful milk
1 teaspoonful caster sugar	1 teaspoonful mixed spice	1 tablespoonful caster sugar
15g/ ½ oz fresh yeast, or 2	25g/1oz caster sugar	
teaspoonfuls dried yeast	25g/1oz butter	
200ml/6fl oz milk, warmed	1 egg, beaten	
to hand-hot		

Pre-heat the oven to 220°C/425°F/Gas Mark 7. Grease a round cake tin about 15cm (6 inches) deep with melted butter, then line the base and the sides with greaseproof paper. Place the batter ingredients in a large mixing bowl and beat with a wooden spoon until a smooth batter is formed. Cover with a cloth and leave in a warm place until it is frothy, about 20-30 minutes. When the batter is ready, add the dough ingredients, and beat well until is it smooth. Pour the mixture into the prepared cake tin, cover and leave in a warm place until it has doubled in size. Uncover, and bake in the pre-heated oven until the cake has risen and the top is golden brown. If the top is browning too quickly, cover it with a piece of greaseproof paper. Just before the cake is ready, make the glaze: heat the milk and sugar together in a small saucepan until the sugar has dissolved, then bring to the boil. Remove the cake from the oven, turn out onto a wire rack, and brush the top of the cake with the glaze immediately, whilst the cake is still hot. When cool, cut the cake across, horizontally, into three sections. Spread the bottom and the middle section with clotted or whipped cream, then sandwich all the pieces together, and cut into slices to serve. Alternatively, the cake can be left in one piece and served in slices, buttered if liked.

— . —

Netherbury, Haymaking by St Mary's Church 1912
65068x

RECIPE

—·—

Saffron Cake

Saffron is derived from the dried and powdered stigmas of the styles of the saffron crocus. It is one of the most expensive spices, as it requires many thousands of crocus flowers to make a small quantity of saffron. It has long been a popular flavouring in both Devon and Cornwall, giving cakes or loaves a golden colour and a honey-like taste. Saffron cakes or buns were once traditionally only made at Easter.

75g/3oz caster sugar
300ml/ ½ pint warm water
2 teaspoonfuls of dried yeast
450g/1 lb strong plain flour
1 teaspoonful salt
A good pinch of saffron
115g/4oz lard
115g/4oz currants or raisins
75g/3oz butter or margarine
Beaten egg, to glaze

Dissolve 1 teaspoonful of the caster sugar in the warm water, add the yeast and mix well, then leave in a warm place until it has become frothy. Sieve the flour, salt and saffron together, then rub in 15g/ ½ oz of the lard. Gradually add in the yeast mixture, and work it all together to make a firm dough. Knead the dough on a floured surface for 10 minutes or so until it has become smooth and elastic. Put the dough in bowl covered with a damp cloth and leave to 'prove' in a warm place until it has doubled in size. When the dough has risen, melt the remaining lard and the butter or margarine together. Work the melted fats, the remaining sugar and the dried fruit into the dough, and knead it all for a further 10 minutes. Leave the dough in a covered bowl in a warm place for a further 30 minutes, until it has risen again.

Pre-heat the oven to 190°C/375°F/Gas Mark 5.

Turn the dough into a well-greased 1kg/2 lb loaf tin, and brush the top of the cake with beaten egg. Bake in the pre-heated oven for 40-45 minutes, or until it is risen and cooked through – cover the top with foil if its starts to brown too much.

Leave in the tin for about 15 minutes before turning out on to a wire tray to cool. Store in an airtight container and serve sliced, spread with butter. This also makes excellent toast.

—·—

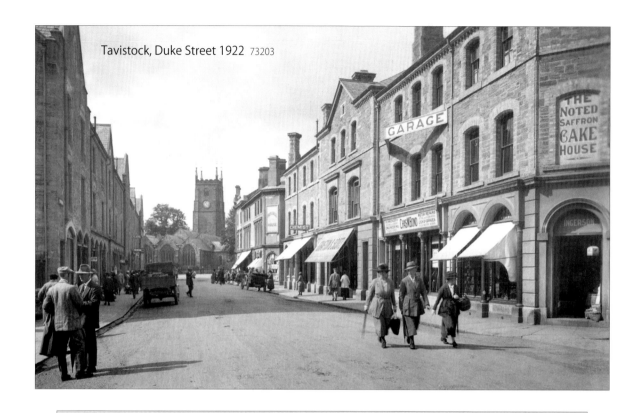

Tavistock, Duke Street 1922 73203

Dialect Words and Phrases From Devon

'Aughts' - leftovers from meals.

'Chilliferous' - extremely cold.

'Crams' - nonsense or tantrums.

'Dimpsy' - dusk, the early evening when it is getting dark.

'Dabbry' - droopy, wilted, floppy.

'Frawzy' - a treat, as in 'Ev yerself a frawzy'.

'Lalager' - tongue.

'Larrupin' - a good thumping, as in 'Stop, or I'll give 'e a gud larrapin'.

'Mitching' - playing truant.

'Tiflin' - loose thread on clothing.

'Wallage' - a heap or pile of something'.

'Zimzoiled' - ruined, spoiled.

RECITE

— · —

Devonshire Splits

These yeasted buns are served split open and filled with Devonshire clotted cream and jam. If served with clotted cream and black treacle they are known as 'Thunder and Lightning'.

15g/½oz fresh yeast, or 10g/¼oz dried yeast
Half a teaspoonful of caster sugar
150ml/¼ pint tepid water
75g/3oz butter or margarine
6 tablespoonfuls of milk
450g/1 lb plain flour
Pinch of salt
Icing sugar to finish
Clotted cream and jam to serve

Sprinkle the yeast and sugar over the tepid water and leave in a warm place until it is frothy. Put the butter or margarine and milk into a small saucepan and heat gently until the fat has melted – do not allow to boil. Remove from heat and allow to cool.

Sift the flour and salt into a mixing bowl, make a well in the centre and pour in the yeast and milk mixtures, then mix the dough until it is soft but not sticky. Turn onto a floured surface and knead gently for 5 minutes, then put into a bowl and leave covered in a warm place for 1 hour.

Take out and knead again a little, then shape into about 18 small balls. Place them on a greased baking sheet a little apart, and leave until they have spread and are just touching.

Bake in a pre-heated oven (200°C/400°F/ Gas Mark 6) for about 20 minutes, or until well risen. When cooked, they should sound hollow when tapped. Dust with icing sugar, and serve split open, spread with clotted cream and jam.

— · —

RECIPE

~ · ~

Devonshire Flats

225g/8oz self-raising flour

115/4oz caster sugar

115ml/3½ fl oz Devonshire clotted or double cream

1 beaten egg

1 tablespoonful milk

Pre-heat the oven to 190°C/375°F/ Gas Mark 5.

Mix the flour and sugar together. Stir in the cream and beaten egg and mix thoroughly with enough milk to make a stiff dough. Roll out the dough very thinly and cut into rounds of about 8cm (3 inches) in diameter. Sprinkle with a little sugar and bake in the pre-heated oven for about ten minutes, until lightly risen and golden brown.

~ · ~

Ashburton, East Street and Bull Ring 1922 73181

RECIPE

—·—

Fairings

Fairings are small, spicy, crunchy biscuits that used to be sold all over the West Country at fairs.

> 225g/8oz self-raising flour
> 1½ teaspoonfuls bicarbonate of soda
> A pinch of salt
> 1 teaspoonful ground ginger
> 1 teaspoonful ground mixed spice
> Half a teaspoonful ground cinnamon
> 115g/4oz butter
> 50g/2oz sugar
> 115g/4oz golden syrup

Pre-heat the oven to 190°C/375°F/Gas Mark 5.

Sift the flour, bicarbonate of soda, salt and spices together, and mix well. Rub in the butter until the mixture resembles fine breadcrumbs, then add the sugar and mix well. Warm the golden syrup a little, then pour it into the mixture, and knead it until it has formed a firm dough. Flour your hands, then roll small amounts of the dough into balls about the size of an egg, and put the balls onto a greased baking tray, well spaced out. Flatten each ball down well with the back of a spoon. Bake in the pre-heated oven for about 10 minutes, or until golden brown. Remove from the oven and cool on a wire rack.

—·—

Trowbridge, Silver Street and Town Hall 1900 45343

RECIPE

— . —

Heavy Cake

Heavy Cake is a Cornish recipe for a slab of fruit cake which is scored on the top to resemble a fishing net. The name may derive from the 'Heva!' call of the Huer, the man on look-out duty on the cliffs watching for shoals of fish, although another theory is that is comes from the 'Heave!' call of the fishermen as they hauled in the seine net to the shore. When the women heard this sound, they knew the men would soon be home for tea, and would make this quick cake.

225g/8oz plain flour
¼ teaspoonful of salt
50g/2oz margarine
75g/3oz sugar
175g/6oz currants
2-3 tablespoonfuls of milk
50g/2oz butter, cut into small pieces

Pre-heat the oven to 200°C/400°F/Gas Mark 6.

Mix the flour and salt in a bowl, and rub in the margarine. Add the sugar and currants, and enough milk to enable the mixture to form a soft dough. Roll out on a floured surface into a long strip. Dot half the butter over the first two-thirds of the dough. Fold the bottom third (without the butter) upwards, then fold the top third down over it. Give the dough a half-turn, so that the folds are now at the sides, and roll out again into a thin strip, dot with butter and fold again in the same way as before.

Roll out into a square about 1cm (½ inch) thick. Score the top with a sharp knife to make a diamond pattern, like a fishing net. Brush with a little milk, place on a greased and floured baking tray above the middle of the pre-heated oven, and bake for about 30 minutes.

— . —

Torquay, Hauling in the Nets 1888 21444

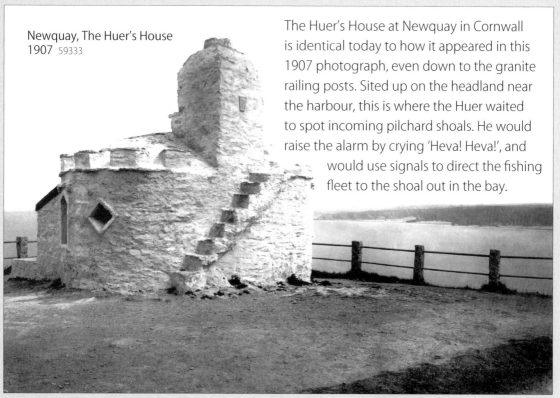

Newquay, The Huer's House
1907 59333

The Huer's House at Newquay in Cornwall is identical today to how it appeared in this 1907 photograph, even down to the granite railing posts. Sited up on the headland near the harbour, this is where the Huer waited to spot incoming pilchard shoals. He would raise the alarm by crying 'Heva! Heva!', and would use signals to direct the fishing fleet to the shoal out in the bay.

RECImpE

—.—

Clifton Puffs

The suburb of Clifton in Bristol is known for its elegant Regency crescents and Georgian terraces. Royal York Crescent, overlooking the Avon Gorge and Brunel's famous suspension bridge, is the largest crescent in England. This recipe makes about 20 Clifton Puffs.

> 1 packet puff pastry
> 1 egg, beaten, to glaze
> Sugar, for dusting
> For the filling:
> 225g/8oz eating apples, peeled, cored and finely chopped
> 225g/8oz currants
> 115g/4oz raisins
> 1 cup chopped candied peel
> 2 cups blanched chopped almonds
> Half a teaspoonful grated nutmeg
> 4-6 tablespoonfuls brandy

Mix all the filling ingredients well together, cover and leave in a warm place for about one hour for the flavours to infuse. Then roll out the pastry very thinly and cut into 10cm (4 inch) squares. Put some of the mixture on one half of each square, dampen the edges and fold over cornerwise, making triangles. Brush with beaten egg, dust with sugar and bake in a pre-heated hot oven (200°C/400°F/Gas Mark 6) for about 15-20 minutes, or until the pastry is risen and a pale gold. These are best served warm.

—.—

Clifton, The Bridge
1887 20164

West Country Cider

Think of the West Country, and most people immediately associate this area with cider. The secret of making good traditional cider is in the blending of juice from several varieties of cider apples, many of which go by delightful names such as Slack-ma-girdle, Honey String, Buttery Door, and Poor Man's Profit.

In his 'View of Devonshire' written in 1630, Thomas Westcote mentions the abundance of Devon orchards, particularly for the making of cider which he describes as being 'a drink both pleasant and healthy, much desired of seamen for long southern voyages as more fit to make beverage than beer, and much cheaper and easier to be had than wine.' Cider was a popular drink both at home and abroad; by 1820 11,265 hogsheads (each holding 63 gallons) of cider were shipped out from the ports of Exeter and Dartmouth.

Cider drinking was widely supposed to promote longevity, and was considered to help prevent scurvy. It was taken on sea voyages for this reason, before the days of lemon and lime juice. John Huxham in 1738 thought that the good health of many people in Devon could be attributed to the popularity of the drink.

The area around Taunton in Somerset was being advertised as 'cider country' as early as 1584, and for many centuries cider production was a key factor in the local economy. In 1894 over 24,000 acres of land around Taunton were being used as orchards. The Taunton Cider Company was set up in 1921 at Norton Fitwarren to make cider on a commercial basis. The company expanded, acquiring other local cider-making companies, and is particularly known for Dry Blackthorn cider. Sadly, cider is no longer made at Norton Fitzwarren, as the company was bought out by Matthew Clark. However, traditional farmhouse cider is still made in Somerset by small-scale producers, and is well worth seeking out.

In most cider-making counties of England a traditional ceremony was held every year which was known as 'wassailing' (from the Anglo-Saxon words 'Waes Hal', meaning 'good health'). Wassailing took place in the winter, usually on Twelfth Night; jugs of cider were carried into the orchards, most of which would be drunk, and the rest would be poured around the roots of the apple trees. A lot of noise would be made with banging of pots and pans, to drive away evil spirits from the trees, and wake up the trees for the spring; sometimes shotguns would be fired through the branches. Special cakes would often be eaten, and pieces of cake or bread, soaked in cider, would be placed in the trees as a thanksgiving to the tree spirit, and to ensure a good crop in the following year.

RECIPE

—·—

Cider Cake

225g/8oz mixed sultanas, raisins and currants

4 tablespoonfuls sweet cider

175g/6oz butter or margarine

175g/6oz soft brown sugar

3 eggs

225g/8oz self-raising flour

1 teaspoonful mixed spice (optional)

Soak the mixed fruits in the cider overnight. Cream the butter or margarine and add the sugar. Cream until fluffy. Lightly beat the eggs and gradually beat them into the mixture. Mix in the fruit and cider. Sift the flour and spice together, fold in half of the flour, and mix well. Mix in the rest of the flour. Grease a 20cm (8 inch) round or 18cm (7 inch) square tin and line the bottom with greased, greaseproof paper. Bake in a pre-heated moderate oven, 180°C/350°C/Gas Mark 4, for 1 hour and 10 minutes.

Old apple tree, we wassail thee, and
hoping thou wilt bear
Hat-fulls, cap-fulls, three bushel bagfulls
And a little heap under the stairs –
Hip! Hip! Hooray!

—·—

INDEX OF PHOTOGRAPHS

INDEX OF RECIPES

Corsham, Box Tunnel 1904 51492

FREE PRINT OF YOUR CHOICE

Mounted Print
Overall size 14 x 11 inches (355 x 280mm)

Choose any Frith photograph in this book.
Simply complete the Voucher opposite and
return it with your remittance for £3.50 (to cover
postage and handling) and we will print the
photograph of your choice in SEPIA (size 11 x 8
inches) and supply it in a cream mount with a
burgundy rule line (overall size 14 x 11 inches).
Please note: aerial photographs and
photographs with a reference number
starting with a "Z" are not Frith photographs
and cannot be supplied under this offer.
Offer valid for delivery to one UK address only.

PLUS: **Order additional Mounted Prints
at HALF PRICE - £9.50 each** (normally £19.00)
If you would like to order more Frith prints from
this book, possibly as gifts for friends and family,
you can buy them at half price (with no
additional postage and handling costs).

PLUS: **Have your Mounted Prints framed**
For an extra £18.00 per print you can have your
mounted print(s) framed in an elegant polished
wood and gilt moulding, overall size
16 x 13 inches (no additional postage and
handling required).

IMPORTANT!

These special prices are only available if you use
this form to order. You must use the ORIGINAL
VOUCHER on this page (no copies permitted). We
can only despatch to one UK address. This offer
cannot be combined with any other offer.

Send completed Voucher form to:
**The Francis Frith Collection, Frith's Barn,
Teffont, Salisbury, Wiltshire SP3 5QP**

CHOOSE A PHOTOGRAPH FROM THIS BOOK

Voucher for **FREE** and Reduced Price *Frith Prints*

*Please do not photocopy this voucher. Only the original is valid,
so please fill it in, cut it out and return it to us with your order.*

Picture ref no	Page no	Qty	Mounted @ £9.50	Framed + £18.00	Total Cost £
		1	Free of charge*	£	£
			£9.50	£	£
			£9.50	£	£
			£9.50	£	£
			£9.50	£	£
			£9.50	£	£

*Please allow 28 days
for delivery.
Offer available to one
UK address only*

* Post & handling	£3.50
Total Order Cost	£

Title of this book . . . .
I enclose a cheque/postal order for £ . . . .
made payable to 'The Francis Frith Collection'

OR please debit my Mastercard / Visa / Maestro card,
details below

Card Number

Issue No (Maestro only)   Valid from (Maestro)

Expires   Signature

Name Mr/Mrs/Ms . . . .
Address . . . .
. . . .
. . . .
. . . . Postcode . . . .
Daytime Tel No . . . .
Email . . . .

978-1-84589-434-4   Valid to 31/12/11

Free Print – see overleaf